The Jones Family

LOLEK

The Boy Who Became
Pope John Paul II

Mary Hramiec Hoffman
Mark Hoffman

HRAMIEC HOFFMAN ™

HRAMIEC HOFFMAN PUBLISHING
HARBOR SPRINGS, MICHIGAN U.S.A.

All inquiries should be addressed to:
Hramiec Hoffman Publishing, a division of Hramiec Hoffman, Inc.
6911 M-119
Harbor Springs, MI 49740
http://www.hramiechoffman.com

Hramiec Hoffman is a registered trademark

Publisher's Cataloging-in-Publication Data

Hoffman, Mary Hramiec.
Lolek : the boy who became Pope John Paul II / Mary Hramiec Hoffman
and Mark Hoffman. – Harbor Springs, Mich. : Hramiec Hoffman Pub., 2009.

p. ; cm.

ISBN13: 978-0-9746901-1-7
ISBN10: 0-9746901-1-2

1. John Paul II, Pope, 1920-2005—Juvenile literature. 2.
Popes—Biography—Juvenile literature. I. Hoffman, Mark, 1963- II.
Title.

BX1378.5 .H64 2008
282.092—dc22   2008929933

Project coordination by Jenkins Group, Inc
www.BookPublishing.com

Printed in Singapore

13 12 11 10 09 • 5 4 3 2 1

For Mark, with all my love.
For my family, especially Dad who loved Pope John Paul II and the Blessed Mother so,
and for Mom who inspires the emulation of Mary in our daily lives.
-Mary Hramiec Hoffman

For Mary who continues to inspire me with her selflessness.
For my Mom and Dad, with sincere thanks for instilling within me a deep faith in God.
-Mark J. Hoffman

Once upon a time there was a little boy named Karol Josef Wojtyla (voy-ti-wah). His friends and family affectionately called him "Lolek." He was born on May 18, 1920, in Wadowice (vah-doe-vee-chay), Poland, which is a small town surrounded by the Tatras Mountains in the beautiful Skawa river valley. His home was small and plain. There was one bedroom where his mom and dad slept, a kitchen, and a parlor where he and his brother slept at night. His mother was a homemaker who used to be a schoolteacher, and his father was a lieutenant in the Polish army.

EMILIA-MOTHER
MARCH 26, 1884-APRIL 13, 1929

KAROL SR.-FATHER
JULY 18, 1879-FEBRUARY 18, 1941

EDMUND-BROTHER
AUGUST 27, 1906-DECEMBER 4, 1932

OLGA-BABY SISTER
1914-1914

KAROL-"LOLEK"
MAY 18, 1920-APRIL 2, 2005

OLGA-NEWBORN SISTER
APRIL 13, 1929-APRIL 13, 1929

TOTUS TUUS

WOJTYLA FAMILY TREE

Poland is surrounded by seven
different countries, and along the
northwest portion of the nation
lies the magnificent Baltic Sea.
World War I ended in 1919, and as
a result, Poland was a free country
for the first time in over 140 years.
Although Lolek was fortunate to
have been born during this time
of exciting independence, the
results of the war took a lot of
power away from some countries
and made their leaders uneasy,
especially Germany's.

One of Lolek's best childhood friends was Jerzy Kluger. Lolek was Catholic, and Jerzy was Jewish. Many people in Poland and across Europe were making Jewish families sad and scared because of their religion. Some people were afraid to be seen with Jews. Although he was only a boy, Lolek knew this was wrong and stood up for his friend. He even played on Jerzy's soccer team. His noble actions were only a glimpse of what the future held for Lolek, who would go on to become one of the greatest leaders in the world, Pope John Paul II.

Playing sports helped Lolek learn about the importance of teamwork, discipline, and sacrifice. He realized that just because people have different beliefs or ideas doesn't mean they can't be an important part of a team. As a result, Lolek had many friends who admired him.

He was also a brilliant student who loved to learn. Lolek could speak three languages by the time he was fourteen, and he grew up to master eight different languages! This made it easy for him to speak to people in the many, many different countries he visited when he became pope.

Lolek's parents instilled in him a deep faith in God. Their apartment was across the street from St. Mary's Cathedral, where he was an altar boy. He was baptized there as a baby and it is where he celebrated one of his first masses after becoming a priest. Lolek celebrated his first communion at St. Mary's too, but that was both a happy and a sad day for him. His mother had died three weeks before that very special event (while giving birth to his baby sister Olga). Lolek was eight years old.

totus tuus

Lolek had a special place in his heart for the Blessed Mother. He would often pray to her in times of need. His father took him and his brother Edmund to a favorite shrine (Kalwaria Zebrzydowska) after their mother died. As Lolek prayed at an image of Mary with baby Jesus, a Latin phrase popped into his head, "Totus tuus," meaning "I am all yours." This was how he felt about his family and God. Some of the sadness left his heart, and at that point the Virgin Mary became more important to Lolek than ever before. Even though his mother was in heaven, he was comforted by the knowledge that Mary was always there to guide him.

"TOTUS TUUS" IS HIDDEN ON MANY PAGES OF THIS STORY!

One of Lolek's favorite things to do when he wasn't studying was to go skiing in the beautiful Tatras Mountains near his home. He and his friends also played hockey on the frozen Skawa River in the winter and swam daringly in its waters in the warm summer months. His adventurous spirit was an important part of his growth. By picturing change and seeking challenges, he excelled and saw that he could do things that others thought were impossible.

totus tuus

The people in Lolek's community were hard workers. On market day, they would sell their vegetables and crafts in the town square. They stayed busy in the winter making useful crafts of wood, embroidery, and clay with traditional folk patterns, crafts that had been passed down for hundreds of years. "Polish pottery" is still prized and collected all over the world, and mostly comes from a town northwest of Lolek's hometown of Wadowice.

Lolek and his town always thanked God for their bountiful crops. They did this by celebrating the Feast of our Lady of the Harvest held each year around August 15, on Assumption Day. Everyone looked forward to this annual gathering of people from all the surrounding towns and villages. The sense of community in Lolek's hometown had a lasting effect on him. This sense broadened to include the whole world as he grew older and embraced different cultures and races. His father taught him that we are all God's children and need to work together to make our world a better place for everyone.

June 23, St. John's Eve, was always special. On this day, the townspeople of Wadowice and all of Poland celebrated God's creation of fire and water. Lolek would go down to the river with his friends and family for a special celebration. Bonfires were lit along the Skawa River's edge and young men would jump over them. Girls wove pretty flowers, herbs, and ribbons into wreaths with candles lit in the center and set them afloat. After the sun went down, the river was very beautiful. These celebrations of gratitude for God's goodness fed a fire burning in Lolek's heart—a fire burning with desire to serve the poor and suffering.

One spring day, Lolek was hiking in the mountains with his father and Jerzy. All of a sudden a thick fog came over the mountain and the boys could not see the trail. They realized they had fallen behind Lolek's father and he was too far ahead to hear them calling. Strange noises came from all sides, and the wind rattled the branches of the trees around them. Frightened and cold, Lolek dropped to his knees and prayed. He soon felt brave and secure knowing that the Lord was always by his side. The fog lifted and the boys found their way back to the Wojtyla home, where Lolek's father was anxiously waiting with hot cocoa for them. This was one of many experiences that confirmed the young boy's knowledge that strength comes from faith.

Lolek's faith was strengthened many times throughout his young life. His beloved older brother Edmund died from scarlet fever three years after their mother died. Lolek's father, deeply saddened, explained that sad things, too, are in God's plan and that they must have faith in Him. Lolek often wondered what God's true plan for him was. He had many interests at which he excelled, including acting. Lolek loved to speak before crowds, and theater prepared him for his work later in life.

Lolek wrote many poems, plays, and books in his lifetime. Two of his plays were turned into films, and an album—a ten-track collection of the pope's poems—was set to music and reached number one on the Polish music charts.

As Lolek became a young man, he struggled to understand how anyone could hate others because of their beliefs. He dreamed of a world where children could grow up in peace. In 1939, the German Nazis invaded his Polish homeland. This marked the beginning of World War II and changed everything, including his interest in becoming an actor. He decided to become a priest instead and was forced to study in a secret seminary at night.

The people of Poland experienced horrible hardships because of the war. All the Jewish people and some of the Catholics were taken away to German extermination camps. Lolek was forced to do very hard work splitting rocks in a stone quarry. If it had been discovered that he was studying to become a priest, he would have been killed, but his faith and good attitude carried him through these terrible times.

Lolek's hard work paid off. He became a priest, amazingly, under a godless, communist government. He continued to study hard and earned two master's degrees and a doctorate, eventually becoming the archbishop of Krakow (Krak uv), a large city northeast of his hometown. Within a few years, he was made a cardinal by the pope. When Pope John Paul I died, Karol "Lolek" Josef Wojtyla was elected to the highest ranking position in the Catholic church, that of pope. The year was 1978, and he was 58 years old. He chose the name Pope John Paul II as a tribute to the pope before him. Lolek was the first slavic pope and the first non-Italian pope in 450 years!

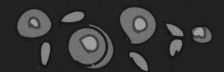

Greenland

Iceland

Canada

Pacific
Ocean

United
States

Atlantic
Ocean

Mexico

South
America

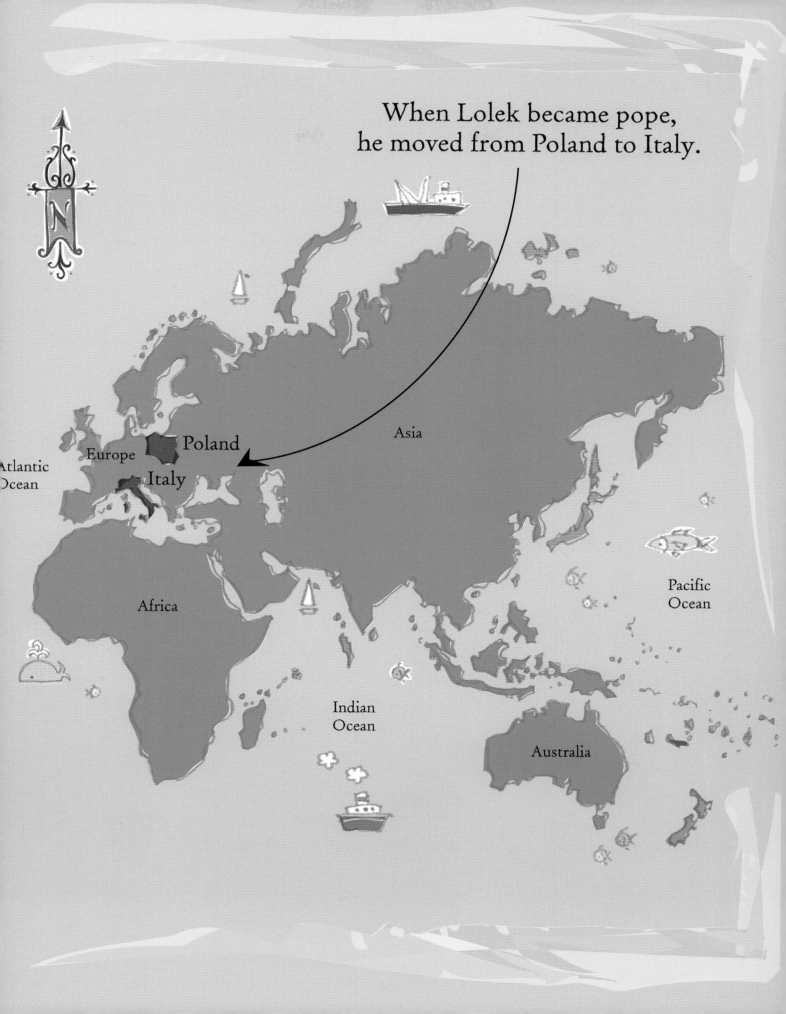

When Lolek became pope,
he moved from Poland to Italy.

He quickly
learned to enjoy many
different things
about his new home,
including the food!

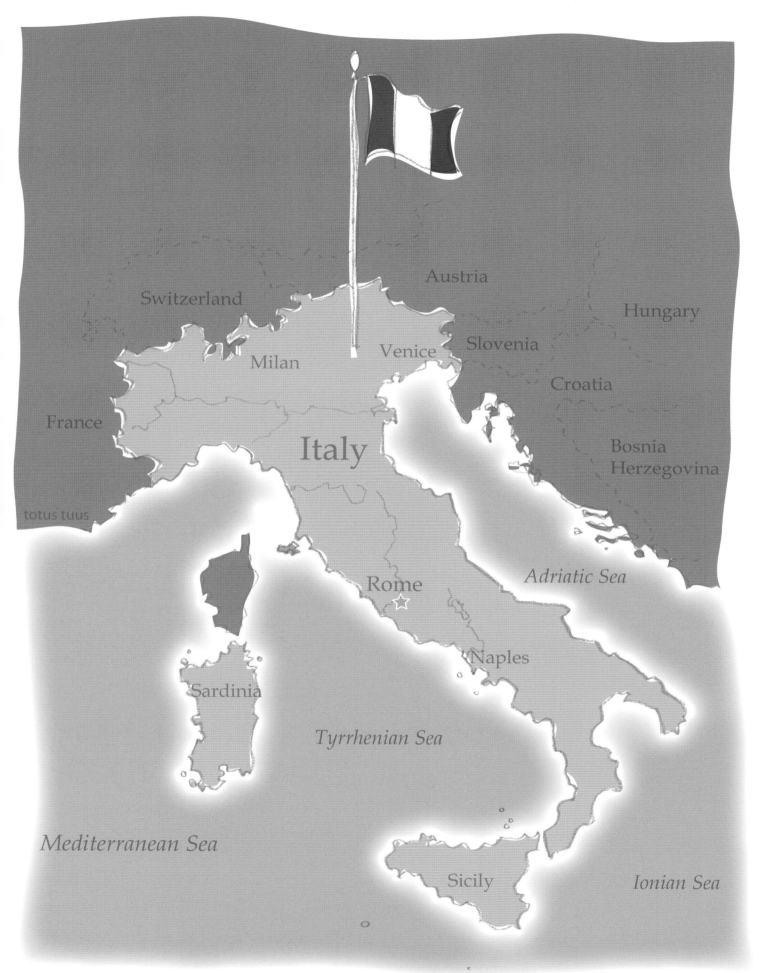

Switzerland

Austria

Hungary

France

Milan

Venice

Slovenia

Croatia

Italy

Bosnia
Herzegovina

totus tuus

Rome

Adriatic Sea

Sardinia

Naples

Tyrrhenian Sea

Mediterranean Sea

Sicily

Ionian Sea

St. Peter's Basilica, in Vatican City,
became Lolek's new home. The basilica
is a big church that can hold over 60,000
people! St. Peter was the very first pope,
and Vatican City is a town inside the
bigger city of Rome, the capital of Italy.
Vatican City is considered an
independent country and has its own
governor, post office, and zip code.

St. Peter's Basilica
Vatican City, Rome, Italy

One of the first things Pope John Paul II did was create his coat of arms. A coat of arms is an arrangement of symbols, usually shown on and around a shield, that tell about somebody's ancestry and interests. Pope John Paul II's coat of arms has St. Peter's keys symbolizing Jesus' gift to Peter of the keys to heaven and the letter "M" to show his devotion to the Blessed Mother Mary.

Your family's last name might have its own coat of arms. If it doesn't, you can create one by making a shield with drawings of your family's values and interests in and around it.

Pope John Paul II was very good at his new job. He travelled around the world fighting for freedom, campaigning for peace, and combatting poverty. Upon his arrival in a new country, he always kissed the ground to show his love and respect. In the 129 countries that he visited during his papacy, he taught that everybody is precious no matter what country they are from, what their religious beliefs are, and whether they are rich or poor, young or old. One of Lolek's greatest achievements was the downfall of Communism in Europe. He encouraged people to feel their own power, and the power of faith led to the freedom of half a continent.

Pope John Paul II was so loved and admired around the world that millions of people, Catholic and non-Catholic alike, flocked to hear his empowering words. Huge adoring crowds met him wherever he went and embarrassed the communist governments, who officially did not believe in God. The communists had forced Catholic churches to close and told people there was no God. Through Pope John Paul II's encouragement, brave people opened the churches and continued to pray. One crowd numbered over one million people, and he told them, "You are men. You have dignity. Don't crawl on your bellies." This was the beginning of the downfall of Communism in Europe. <u>Time</u> magazine, in naming him Man of the Year, noted that he generated an electricity "unmatched by anyone else on earth."

totus tuus

Pope John Paul II didn't just take care of church affairs, he made the world's business his business, especially when it came to human rights. His great hope was to awaken the entire world to the dignity and responsibility of defending human rights and his criticism of evil dictators encouraged opposition movements that eventually brought down those governments. On June 4, 2004, Pope John Paul II was awarded the Presidential Medal of Freedom by George W. Bush, America's highest civilian honor.

totus tuus

"Your Holiness," said the president to Pope John Paul II, "greetings from the United States of America, where you are respected, admired, and greatly loved.

We will work for human liberty and human dignity, in order to spread peace and compassion; we appreciate the strong symbol of freedom that you have stood for, and we recognize the power of freedom to change societies and to change the world. You have given courage to others to be not afraid in overcoming injustice and oppression. Your stand for peace and freedom has inspired millions and helped to topple Communism and tyranny. The United States honors this son of Poland who became the Bishop of Rome and a hero of our time."

"Thank you, Mr. President," the pope replied. "May the desire for freedom, peace, and a more humane world symbolized by this medal inspire everyone in the world.

God bless America."

George W. Bush presenting Pope John Paul II
with the Presidential Medal of Freedom

What are your gifts? What do you need to do
to overcome obstacles and be the best person
that you can be?

Pope John Paul II
Karol "Lolek" Josef Wojtyla
May 18, 1920–April 2, 2005

Pope John Paul II told us not to be afraid, so we look to the future with hope, joy, love, and the expectation of life hereafter. He left a shining light that will never fail through any darkness in our lives. His fearlessness and courage will forever be a reminder to us at times when we must show courage, steadfastness, and love. His powerful words are tools that guide us in all that we do. For these reasons, he is loved by all and is a saint in all of our hearts.

As Lolek demonstrated, it takes years of study and prayer to become a pope. First, a young man must spend a year praying. Next, he goes to school to learn theology (the study of religion) in a seminary, which is a special school just for learning to become a priest. He must study until he receives a college degree in the seminary. Young women go through similar schooling to become nuns. Someone thinking about becoming a priest or a nun should be able to live in a community—in a house with other priests or nuns. They must really love other people and they must be creative and work well with others. Above all, God must be very important to them. If your heart is calling you to religious work, talk to a priest or nun and ask for guidance.

SEMINARIAN

PRIEST

BISHOP

CARDINAL

POPE

THE SIGN OF THE CROSS
In the name of the Father,
And of the Son,
And of the Holy Spirit.
Amen.

THE APOSTLES' CREED
I believe in God, the Father almighty,
creator of heaven and earth.
I believe in Jesus Christ, his only Son, our Lord.
He was conceived by the power of the Holy Spirit
and born of the Virgin Mary.
He suffered under Pontius Pilate,
was crucified, died, and was buried.
He descended into hell.
On the third day he rose again.
He ascended into heaven, and is seated at the right hand
of the Father.
He will come again to judge the living and the dead.
I believe in the Holy Spirit,
the holy Catholic Church,
the communion of saints,
the forgiveness of sins, the resurrection of the body,
and the life everlasting
Amen.

THE LORD'S PRAYER (OUR FATHER)
Our Father, who art in heaven,
hallowed be thy name;
thy kingdom come
thy will be done
on earth as it is in heaven.
Give us this day our daily bread;
and forgive us our trespasses
as we forgive those who trespass against us;
and lead us not into temptation,
but deliver us from evil.
Amen.

HAIL MARY
Hail Mary, full of grace.
The Lord is with thee.
Blessed art thou among women,
and blessed is the fruit of thy womb, Jesus.
Holy Mary, Mother of God,
pray for us sinners,
now and at the hour of our death.
Amen.

THE GLORY BE (THE DOXOLOGY)
Glory be to the Father,
and to the Son,
and to the Holy Spirit.
As it was in the beginning,
is now, and ever shall be,
world without end.
Amen.

FATIMA INVOCATION
O my Jesus, forgive us our sins, save us from the fires of
hell, and lead all souls to heaven, especially those most in
need of thy mercy.

HAIL HOLY QUEEN (SALVE REGINA)
Hail, holy Queen, Mother of mercy. Hail, our life, our
sweetness, and our hope. To you do we cry, poor
banished children of Eve. To you do we send up our
sighs, mourning and weeping in this valley of tears.
Turn then, most gracious advocate, your eyes of mercy
toward us and after this, our exile, show unto us the
blessed fruit of your womb, Jesus. O clement, O loving,
O sweet Virgin Mary. Pray for us, O holy Mother of
God. That we may be made worthy of the promises of
Christ.

THE JOYFUL MYSTERIES
1. The Annunciation of the birth of the Lord to Mary
by the archangel Gabriel
2. The Visitation of Our Lady with St. Elizabeth, the
mother of St. John the Baptist
3. The Nativity of Our Lord
4. The Presentation of the Christ Child in the Temple
5. The Finding of the Child Jesus in the Temple

THE SORROWFUL MYSTERIES
1. The Agony in the Garden
2. The Scourging of Jesus
3. The Crowning with Thorns
4. The Carrying of the Cross
5. The Crucifixion

THE LUMINOUS MYSTERIES
1. The Baptism of Our Lord in the River Jordan
2. The Self-Manifestation of Our Lord at the Wedding at Cana
3. The Proclamation of the Kingdom of God
4. The Transfiguration of Our Lord
5. The Last Supper, when the Eucharist was Instituted

THE GLORIOUS MYSTERIES
1. The Resurrection
2. The Ascension
3. The Descent of the Holy Spirit at Pentecost
4. The Assumption of the Blessed Virgin Mary
5. The Coronation of the Blessed Mother

totus tuus

POPE JOHN PAUL II
ADDED THESE
MYSTERIES TO THE
ROSARY!

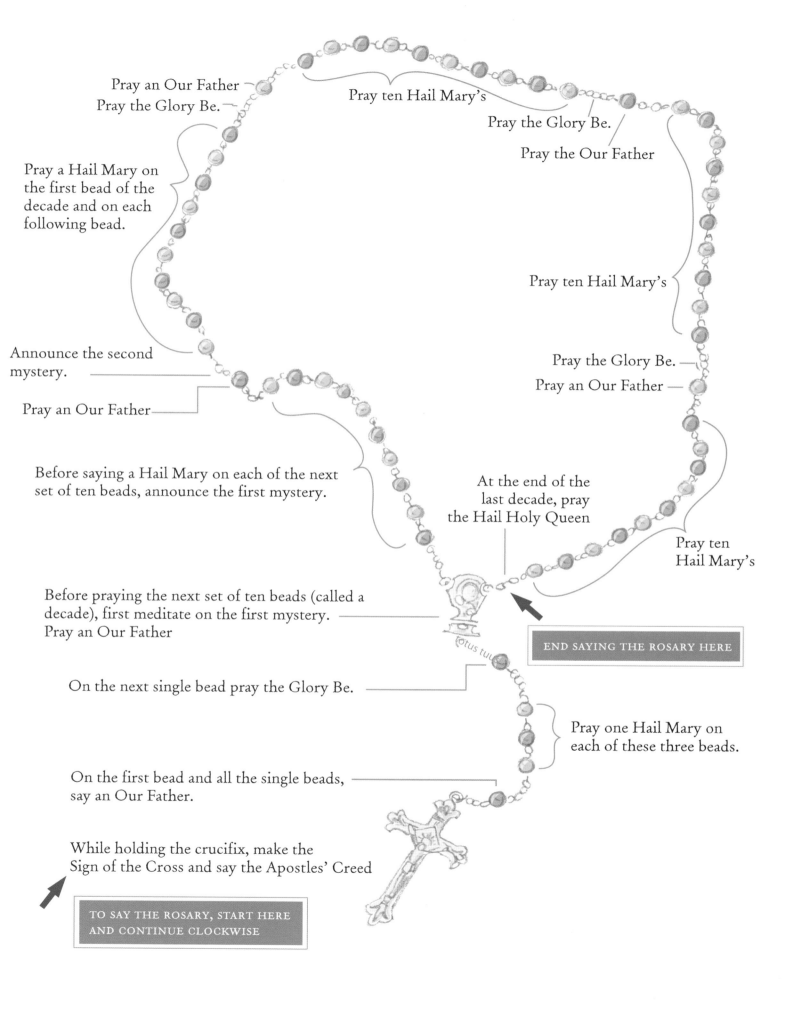

Pray an Our Father
Pray the Glory Be.

Pray ten Hail Mary's

Pray the Glory Be.

Pray the Our Father

Pray a Hail Mary on
the first bead of the
decade and on each
following bead.

Pray ten Hail Mary's

Announce the second
mystery.

Pray the Glory Be.

Pray an Our Father

Pray an Our Father

Before saying a Hail Mary on each of the next
set of ten beads, announce the first mystery.

At the end of the
last decade, pray
the Hail Holy Queen

Pray ten
Hail Mary's

Before praying the next set of ten beads (called a
decade), first meditate on the first mystery.
Pray an Our Father

END SAYING THE ROSARY HERE

On the next single bead pray the Glory Be.

Pray one Hail Mary on
each of these three beads.

On the first bead and all the single beads,
say an Our Father.

While holding the crucifix, make the
Sign of the Cross and say the Apostles' Creed

TO SAY THE ROSARY, START HERE
AND CONTINUE CLOCKWISE

DEAR READER,

The task of researching and assembling this book was a rewarding journey for us. Karol "Lolek" Josef Wojtyla was nothing short of an amazing human being and we are fortunate to have known and loved him as our pope for twenty-six years. Lolek celebrates the childhood of Pope John Paul II and it is our hope that it serves as an inspiration for children and adults cultivating tolerance, gratitude, humility, faith, fortitude, and love for all mankind. Our intention is to induce quiet reverence as well as inspire action in a tribute to our beloved Lolek as human rights advocates and defenders of the oppressed. May we dedicate our lives and souls to the greater good of mankind using the Holy Father as a template.

Many world travelers settle for the summer in the beautiful resort area of Little Traverse Bay on Lake Michigan, where Mary and Mark Hoffman are honored to live and work with their four children.

In addition to the beauty of their surroundings, Mary's creative inspirations emanate from experiences traveling the United States with her parents, seven brothers and sisters, and the family dog in one of America's first motorhomes, one her father expertly fashioned from a GM delivery truck.

Charity has always been important to Mark and Mary. They continue to support cancer research organizations and both national and local charity programs.

Mary produces a multitude of art including original oil paintings and clay art in addition to her line of greeting cards, prints, and books. You are cordially invited to Mark and Mary's fine arts and crafts gallery in Harbor Springs, Michigan, or online.

Hramiec Hoffman Studio & Gallery
6911 M119 Harbor Springs, Michigan 49740
(231) 526-1011
www.hramiechoffman.com

PURCHASE COLLECTIBLES AND DOWNLOAD FREE PAGES FOR LOLEK THE BOY WHO BECAME POPE JOHN PAUL II AT WWW.POPELOLEK.COM